How to Coach
Leadership in a PLC

Marc Johnson

Solution Tree | Press

555 North Morton Street
Bloomington, IN 47404
800.733.6786 (toll free) / 812.336.7700
FAX: 812.336.7790
email: info@solution-tree.com
solution-tree.com
Printed in the United States of America

19 18 17 16 15   1 2 3 4 5

Library of Congress Cataloging-in-Publication Data

Johnson, Marc (Marcus Paul), 1953-

  How to coach leadership in a PLC / by Marc Johnson.

      pages cm. -- (Solutions)

  Includes bibliographical references.

  ISBN 978-1-936764-41-9 (perfect bound) 1. Professional learning communities--California--Sanger. 2. School improvement programs--California--Sanger. 3. Educational change--California--Sanger. 4. Educational leadership--California--Sanger. 5. Sanger Unified School District (Calif.) I. Title.

  LB1731.J558 2015

  371.2'011--dc23

                          2015011361

Solution Tree
Jeffrey C. Jones, CEO
Edmund M. Ackerman, President

Solution Tree Press
President: Douglas M. Rife
Associate Acquisitions Editor: Kari Gillesse
Editorial Director: Lesley Bolton
Managing Production Editor: Caroline Weiss
Copy Editor: Ashante K. Thomas
Proofreader: Elisabeth Abrams
Text and Cover Designer: Rian Anderson
Compositor: Abigail Bowen

Acknowledgments

Having never tried my hand at writing a book, I want to start by thanking Claudia Wheatley for encouraging me to start this adventure. A very special thanks goes to my editor, Kari Gillesse, for her patience with me, even when I made her work twice as hard as she should have had to do!

Thanks to my mom, Rosemary Avants Johnson Manahan, who says she is responsible for everything I have accomplished; that statement is truer than you realize, Mom!

Thanks to my wife, Penni, for standing by me, supporting me, believing in me, and for being my best friend.

Thanks to my kids Alyssa, Mikael, and Ashlea, and my grandkids Derek, Ryan, Aubrey, Ashlyn, and Jeffrey. Thanks for the blessings each of you have been and continue to be to me, and for all that I have learned from you.

Thank you to my Sanger Unified family for sharing the most incredible journey of my life with me, and may you journey on. There is no place on our path called *good enough*; it's *every child, every day, whatever it takes*!

Thanks to Lloyd Kuhn and Rich Smith, the two men who challenged me most in my thinking and never wavered in their support for our work on behalf of kids. What a ride we had!

And finally, to Rick and Becky DuFour: Little did any of us realize the powerful outcomes that would result from those two days in May 2005. You have transformed me as an educator and a leader.

Thank you for your inspiration, mentorship, and, most important of all, your friendship. Your impact on our work in Sanger has been tremendous, and your legacy will forever be connected to the success of our children and that of millions of others. Thank you both for who you are and what you have done!

Table of Contents

About the Author

 **Marc Johnson** is a retired superintendent of the Sanger Unified School District, where he served fourteen years—ten as superintendent. Sanger Unified is located in the heart of California's San Joaquin Valley. Its 10,900 students mirror the demographics of the region: high-minority, high-poverty, and high-English learner (EL) populations. In 2004, shortly after Marc was named superintendent, the district was one of ninety-eight in California to be named a Program Improvement district due to the low performance of the EL population. Two years later, Sanger was one of the first districts in California to exit Program Improvement status due to all its students' continued improvement, but in particular, the improvement of its ELs. The professional learning community (PLC) model served as the catalyst and vehicle for its continuing improvement, and Sanger continues districtwide implementation of the PLC model.

Marc continues his involvement in public education in the Central Valley, where he has served for thirty years. He is currently the co-director of the Central Valley Educational Leadership Institute (CVELI) at California State University, Fresno. He began his career in American Union, a single-school K–8 Fresno County district, where he taught for sixteen years, and also served as junior high vice principal and later as superintendent and principal for seven years. He went to Sanger Unified in 1999 as assistant superintendent for human resources and also served as associate superintendent before being named superintendent in 2003. He worked tirelessly to build and strengthen a culture of collaboration throughout his district. The district's success has generated opportunities for Marc to share Sanger's story throughout the state of California.

Marc received his bachelor's degree in liberal studies from California State University, Fresno, and his master's degree in education with an emphasis in mathematics and science from Fresno Pacific University. Marc and his wife of forty years, Penni, have three children: Alyssa, Mikael, and Ashlea. They also have five grandchildren: Derek, Ryan, Aubrey, Ashlyn, and Jeffrey.

To book Marc Johnson for professional development, contact pd@solution-tree.com.

Introduction

If you don't know where you're going, you might end up someplace else.

—Yogi Berra

On May 5, 2005, over six hundred people gathered in the conference center of a Marriott hotel in Palm Desert, California. Most of the participants were from school districts in Riverside County, California, but four administrators from the Sanger Unified School District in Fresno County sat at a table in the middle of the room. They had made the five-hour journey from the Central Valley to hear Richard and Rebecca DuFour share a two-day presentation about professional learning communities (PLCs). The Sanger team knew that a PLC had six characteristics:

1. Shared mission (our purpose), vision (clear direction), values (collective commitments), goals (indicators, timelines, targets), all of which are focused on student learning

2. A collaborative culture with a focus on learning

3. Collective inquiry into best practice and current reality

4. Action orientation or "learning by doing"

5. A commitment to continuous improvement

6. A results orientation (DuFour, DuFour, Eaker, & Many, 2010; DuFour & Fullan, 2013, p. 14)

Sanger High School had been involved in an ongoing project on school improvement with the Riverside County Office for two years;

as a result of those conversations, they had been working at implementing the PLC model. The presentation confirmed to the Sanger leaders that full commitment to the PLC model was exactly what was needed to frame the work of the entire district. The PLC presentation clarified where we were going and the work we needed to lead.

Sanger Unified is located in the heart of California's San Joaquin Valley. The district covers 180 square miles of mostly rural agricultural land and includes the city of Sanger and several small, unincorporated communities. In 2004, the district served about 9,500 students. The student population included 82 percent minority students with the largest group being Hispanic and growing populations of Southeast Asians and African Americans. Together the district's students speak more than twenty languages, and 24 percent of the students were categorized as English learners (ELs). Over 75 percent of the students qualified for free or reduced lunch, so poverty was and still is a factor throughout the community and district. Another factor that affected the district was the educational status of the students' parents: 28 percent had not graduated from high school, and another 24 percent had graduated high school but never attended college. Forty-nine percent of parents did not speak English as their primary language.

When you consider those statistics, you probably don't find it too surprising that the district struggled with student achievement. That struggle was at the core of the letter that the new assistant superintendent for curriculum and instruction, Rich Smith, received from the California Department of Education in September 2004, notifying the district that it was one of the first ninety-eight districts in California to fall into Program Improvement (PI) status for failing to make adequate yearly progress (AYP). There are over one thousand school districts in California, and this designation was an indicator that the district was in the bottom 10 percent with regards to student achievement. When you look at the root cause for the designation as a district in need of dramatic improvement, one site, Jefferson Elementary, serves as an example.

Jefferson Elementary is a school of 450 students on the east side of Sanger. It is located in an area that has historically been seen as "the wrong side of the tracks," and, actually, that is a literal description as well. A rail line that served the fruit-packing facilities and processing plants—for decades a source of seasonal employment for much of the community—divides the city of Sanger. The neighborhoods on the east side of the tracks include some of the highest levels of poverty and needs in Sanger, and Jefferson was no exception. Jefferson's student population includes 100 percent free and reduced lunch, 99 percent minority enrollment, and 60 percent ELs. In 2002, the state assessment data for Jefferson showed that only 3.3 percent of the ELs (fewer than nine students) had demonstrated proficiency or advanced proficiency in English language arts. Similar results could be found throughout the district, and it was mainly our failure to support the ELs that resulted in our designation as a PI district.

When Rich Smith speaks of the day he got the PI designation, he recalls feeling that, being only four months into his job as assistant superintendent of curriculum and instruction, he had just signed on as first mate on the *Titanic*. Rich and I spent most of that day digging into data and seeking the *whys* behind our status. As we looked at the evidence, we saw blaring indicators that as a system we had failed to recognize and respond to most of our students' learning needs. That day, we made a commitment to each other and to the students that the leaders of the district would find a way to build the structures necessary to support learning for all students, build the capacity to meet those learning needs, and believe that this work was necessary, not because of a compliance-driven label but rather because it was what our students deserved.

The district leaders committed to build awareness across the system of the current reality and to assess status, capacity, and focus. We focused on these questions: Who were the kids in our system who were not doing well? How were we responding to the needs of those children? What do we need (resources, data, professional learning, and capacity building) to develop a better response that will meet the needs of every child? As Sanger's self-assessment progressed, it became obvious that the district as a whole lacked a sense of common intent. It could best be described as a system driven by a series of random acts of self-improvement at the school level with no unifying vision or mission districtwide. That realization was in great part why Rich, two principals, and I had driven to Riverside County that day to hear the DuFours discuss the PLC learning by doing journey. This journey begins with the three big ideas and four key questions that guide the work of a PLC (DuFour et al., 2010):

1. A relentless focus on student learning and a commitment to ongoing job-embedded learning by the adults in the organization

2. The development of a collaborative culture where everyone is part of a high-functioning team that works together interdependently to achieve a common goal while holding one another mutually accountable to commitments and outcomes

3. A results orientation that seeks constant evidence of student learning (data) and then converts these data to information to support the learning of all students and focus the adults' job-embedded learning

The four key questions a PLC uses to focus and guide its work are the simple framework that caught our attention:

1. **What do we want our students to learn?** What are the essential standards that define the guaranteed, viable curriculum that we must provide every student?

2. **How do we know that learning has occurred?** What are the common formative assessment tools and strategies we will use, and what will a successful

student look like when we are done teaching the material?

3. **How will we respond when learning has not occurred?** What are the levels of support we must build to make it harder for a student to fail than to be successful?

4. **How will we respond when learning has occurred?** For those students who already demonstrate mastery, how do we take them deeper and further challenge them?

After delving into these three concepts and four questions to guide our district's improvement, Sanger Unified committed to become a professional learning community. As the sessions continued, it became clear to the team that not only was this the journey we needed to follow, it was a journey that needed to begin as soon as possible.

At the end of the second day's session, Rich and I began the five-hour drive back home to Sanger from Riverside County and talked about the power of what we heard and why PLCs were where the district needed to go. The DuFours had laid out a series of shifts in thinking and actions the district needed to make (adapted from DuFour et al., 2010, pp. 249–251):

- **A shift in fundamental purpose**
  - From a focus on teaching to a focus on learning
  - From emphasis on what was taught to a fixation on what students learned
  - From coverage of content to demonstration of proficiency
- **A shift in use of assessments**
  - From infrequent summative assessments to frequent common formative assessments

- From assessments to determine which students failed to learn by the deadline to assessments to identify students who need additional time and support

- From individual teacher assessments to assessments developed jointly by collaborative teams

- **A shift in response when students don't learn**

  - From individual teachers determining the appropriate response to a systematic response that ensures support for every student

  - From fixed time and support for learning to time and support for learning as variables

  - From remediation to intervention

- **A shift in the work of teachers**

  - From each teacher clarifying what students must learn to collaborative teams building shared knowledge and understanding about essential learning

  - From individual teachers attempting to discover ways to improve results to collaborative teams of teachers helping each other improve

  - From an assumption that these are "my kids and those are your kids" to an assumption that these are "our kids"

- **A shift in focus**

  - From an external focus on the issues outside of the school to an internal focus on the steps the staff can take to improve the school

  - From a focus on inputs to a focus on results

- From teachers gathering data from their individually constructed tests in order to assign grades, to collaborative teams acquiring information from common assessments in order to 1) inform individual and collective practices, and 2) respond to students who need additional time and support

- **A shift in school culture**

  - From independence to interdependence

  - From a language of complaint to a language of commitment

  - From long-term strategic planning to planning for short-term wins

- **A shift in professional development**

  - From external training (workshops and courses) to job-embedded learning

  - From the expectation that learning occurs infrequently (on the few days devoted to professional development) to an expectation that learning is ongoing and occurs as part of routine work practice

  - From learning by listening to learning by doing

While the need to make these shifts in attitude and action was so clear and powerful, so, too, was the realization that committed leadership at all levels would be required to be successful. Richard Elmore (2004) describes what it takes leadership to be successful: "Rather than focusing on the character traits and actions of individual leaders—in the heroic American tradition of charismatic leadership—we will increasingly have to focus on the distribution of leadership" (p. 42). This describes leaders who consistently engage others in the PLC journey and ensure that all students' learning is at the core of our thinking and actions are required at all levels. Activating and developing this kind of leadership requires us to consider the following:

- How do we establish a foundation of effective leadership for PLCs?

- How do we develop and support a system of distributed leadership?

- How do we define leadership roles at the district level, site level, and team level?

- What structures and supports do we need in place to sustain leadership coaching?

- How do we coach leadership capacity of our current leaders to guide the work of PLCs?

These are among the questions this book seeks to answer, as they are questions that must be answered by anyone who embarks on this journey. We explore what leadership looks like, what it requires, and how district and site leaders coach the development of leadership capacity. This book serves as a resource to improve practice and increase effectiveness in leading PLCs.

Chapter 1
Laying the Foundation for PLC Leadership

Our chief want is someone who will inspire us to be what we know we could be.

—Ralph Waldo Emerson

In reflecting on the shifts listed in the introduction, each requires change—change in how we operate, focus, work, and see ourselves. These changes do not happen without effective leadership that communicates a shared purpose, establishes a culture of collaboration, and motivates change.

Communicating a Shared Purpose

The starting point to lead these shifts and a commitment to continuous improvement rest on communicating a shared purpose to all engaged in the PLC. The foundation for PLC work rests on four pillars: (1) mission, (2) vision, (3) values, and (4) goals. Teams question, "Why do we exist?," "What must our school become to accomplish our purpose?," "How must we behave to achieve our vision?," and "How will we mark our progress?" (DuFour et al., 2010).

Leaders at all levels must build shared understanding of these four pillars so that there is alignment of beliefs, focus, and effort. This takes more than a one-time discussion or memo pointing out what is important; it requires clear, consistent reminders throughout the organization that this is who we are, what we stand for, and why we are engaged in this work. I was once reminded of how important it is as a leader to never assume others know what our priorities are. Rich Smith, while Sanger's deputy superintendent, and I were working with a group of superintendents from a neighboring county and their cabinets to develop the focus of their PLC work. On our first day, we asked all of the superintendents to each take three sticky notes and list their three main district goals—the three most important things they were focusing on. We then asked each of their cabinet members to do the same. The superintendents placed their three goals on the table and had the cabinet members place theirs under any of their superintendent's goals if they aligned, and if not, to start a new column. We then asked how many district teams had only three aligned columns of goals. None did! All districts had at least six, and some as many as ten columns, of main goals. The superintendents were shocked at how little clarity there was about the important work of the district. If this lack of common under-standing exists at the cabinet level, what level of discrepancy exists at the site level? Establishing a sense of shared mission, vision, values, and goals is critical to developing the common intent that everyone in the system understands and embraces.

Expressing a Shared Identity

Every member of an organization has his or her own set of inter-nalized beliefs and values as well as a sense of personal identity. Developing a sense of shared identity as an organization requires that despite our personal differences, we all understand the organizational values. At Sanger, shaping the organizational culture was an ongoing project. We coached this shift in culture several ways. Since 2002, no outside voice has led the start-of-the-year general session; instead, the superintendent has led this gathering of all Sanger Unified employees to reflect on accomplishments and review goals for the PLC work ahead. Each year, a theme guides our focus on who we have to be to accomplish our goals.

We start simple and focus on our shared beliefs using John Christensen's (1998) video *FISH!*. This video, based on the work philosophy of Pike Place Fish Market in Seattle, lays out four simple guidelines for how we need to approach our work:

1. Be there!

2. Make their day!

3. Play!

4. Choose your attitude!

We remind ourselves that it is important that we be present every day, not just in attendance, but engaged in our work, present in a very real sense. We have to take the time to validate others and recognize their efforts and contributions to our outcomes. We must find a way to laugh together so that the work we do and the place where we work together combines into something we enjoy. Finally, we remember that the only thing we have control over on any given day is who we choose to be, the attitude we bring to our work. Who we are in front of our students will determine the outcomes for those students that day. We must always be the adult who cares and believes in them; we must choose great—not good—if we hope to see great things happen. Those were expectations of all and a leadership coaching responsibility at all levels to be modeled.

Each year in succession, we continued to add themes to shape our identity. While the themes serve as powerful reminders of our vision and our commitments to one another as well as a great coaching tool for leadership, our guiding principles have become the foundation of our shared values and shape our identity.

Confirming Direction With Guiding Principles

Shortly after our district fell into Program Improvement status, Rich Smith and I discussed the need to develop a clear and consistent message that would help shape our beliefs and drive our actions. Rich focused on three points that we shared with site leaders and the district office team and simplified them to frame what we called our guiding principles:

1. Hope is not a strategy!

2. Don't blame the kids!

3. It's about student learning!

These keystones of our organization were used each year at the general session, on documents, on posters, and as coaching tools for leaders at all levels to use to shape our identity and culture. The principles were simple, but they reinforced a commitment to our beliefs and directed our actions.

We can't hope things get better; it takes the deliberate actions of adults to change things. How many times have you heard someone say, "I sure hope my students do better this year," and yet he or she does what he or she has always done and wonders why the results are the same? If we want to change outcomes, it is our actions that must change.

"If they'd just give me better students, I'd get better results!" Have you ever heard that from a colleague? I have! Yes, it is true, many of our students come to us from a background of poverty, from broken homes, from abusive situations, and from homes where English is not the primary language. These factors and so many more are true about the students we serve. What is also true is that not one of these students chose the condition of life or factors influencing her or him—it is the life into which the student was born. We are the only hope of changing that condition of life; education is the key. Learning for all is the need. We must know our students and respond to their needs by building systems of support around them that ensure their success. We must own the learning of every student!

"I don't know what happened. I taught it; they just didn't learn it!" Again, a comment frequently made but driven by an incorrect assumption. Teaching generates learning; teaching without learning is just presenting. If students didn't learn it, we didn't teach it! We must ensure that all students learn and that learning for all is the outcome of adults' actions in every classroom. To this end, we must also be committed to being learners as well so that we learn from one another as we examine the results of our efforts. We share best practices, and we support one another. The best way for leaders to coach here is to be seen as learners as well, being transparent about results, seeking input from others, and constantly seeking to improve outcomes.

These guiding principles continue to form the core of the beliefs and values that drive the work of Sanger. The questions each of us must answer are: What are those core values, those guiding principles, that must become the leadership message of our organization? What are the messages that help us shape culture and coach the development of a shared identity?

Establishing a Culture of Collaboration

Shaping the culture of our organizations is a daily focus of leadership at all levels on our journey. *Who* we are—our identity and our relationships—must be a focus of our conversations and our actions. I am more convinced than ever that shaping the culture of our organizations is a critical aspect of leadership and one of the least emphasized.

What does it mean to collaborate in PLC work? In a keynote, Rebecca DuFour (2014) notes that "when considering collaboration, it's not a question of. . . Did we spend time together, but rather, did the time we spent together influence our work?" She goes on to say that in the world of PLC work,

> collaboration is defined as "a *systematic* process in which [educators] work together, interdependently, to analyze and *impact* their professional practice in order to improve individual and collective results. (DuFour et al., 2010, p. 120)

So collaboration is, then, focused time a team spends together to learn from results and improve learning outcomes for the students they teach by improving the efforts of the team. It definitely requires that the outcome of the time adults spend together improves student learning. To achieve this impact, we need to understand the concept of *team* in this work. If asked to define the word *team*, most people respond with something close to this: a group of people who work together to achieve a common goal. While this may be a commonly held definition, in the PLC world, we must go deeper. The definition we need to focus on is the one I heard Richard DuFour (2005) share. A team is "a group of people who work together interdependently to achieve a common goal while holding one another mutually accountable." It is this mixed sense of interdependence and mutual accountability that comprises the essential elements of team structure and function. The shift from operating in isolation to functioning as a team is a shift that must be guided and nurtured, and the roles of the team leader in the PLC and site leader supporting the PLCs are critical.

Motivating Change

Leading change is hard work and requires that we understand how to motivate change in others. Michael Fullan (2008) suggests that there are six secrets to change, which leaders must understand to help their organizations change and advance:

1. **Love your employees**—If we build our organizations with a total focus on our customers (students and parents) without making the same careful commitment to our employees, we will not succeed. Our organization's success requires that we invest in building our employees' capacity in relation to high-quality purpose.

2. **Connect peers with purpose**—The job of leaders is to provide good direction while pursuing implementation through purposeful peer interaction in relation to results. Purposeful peer interaction works best when three conditions exist: (1) organizational values are clearly conveyed and embraced by all groups and individuals within the organization, (2) a culture of learning is supported by the sharing of best practices and information throughout the organization, and (3) monitoring systems and structures use data to identify and address ineffective actions while at the same time identifying and integrating effective practices and strategies.

3. **Capacity building prevails**—Capacity building entails leaders investing in the development of individual and collective efficacy of a whole group or system to accomplish significant improvements. In particular, capacity building should include the development of new competencies, new resources (time, ideas, expertise), and new motivation.

4. **Learning is the work**—Learning in isolation from and external to the job can represent a source of useful input, but if it is not in balance and in concert

with job-embedded learning (learning in the setting in which you work), the learning will end up being superficial.

5. **Transparency rules**—Transparency means that there is a clear and continuous display of results and clear and continuous access to practice (what is being done to achieve those results).

6. **Systems learn**—Systems can learn on a continuous basis, and the most powerful and synergistic form of system learning is found in the system that learns from itself. Often systems fail to sustain learning because they are too reliant on a single leader. For systems to learn and sustain that learning, rather than looking to one person to show the way, they work on the development of many leaders within (such as your school or district) to collaboratively develop continuous learning and improvement. Systems learn when the organization is able to face complex challenges with confidence and when they see those challenges as opportunities to learn.

Fullan helps set the stage for understanding leadership at all levels in the work. These six keys can help you establish a sense of what DuFour and Fullan (2013) call *systemness* so that every department and program sees how it is connected to the work of the site and district. We must build solid, professional relationships with respect and trust. These relationships also must be built on a clear understanding of the level of professionalism that is required to work together in an interdependent manner while holding one another mutually accountable for results. That does not mean that we can't be friends—not at all! It means that we can't let friendship get in the way of the work. It is the development of the commitments that we make—our norms—that guides the *professional* relationship.

Building Relationships

When I came to Sanger, I was amazed at how my presence on a site or in a classroom made people nervous. If I visited classrooms, most of the time, the teacher would stop teaching and nervously ask, "Can I help you?" As I learned more about our organizational culture, I learned that superintendent-level central-office members did not visit sites on a regular basis. The assistant superintendent for human resources generally only showed if there was a crisis or someone was in trouble. One teacher later told me, "The first time you walked into my room, I was so nervous because the last time we saw the assistant superintendent on our site was the day they fired our principal!" In order for any member of our central-office team to be effective in a coaching and capacity-building role on site, it was necessary to break that existing culture of fear and us-versus-them mentality.

We had to reestablish trust in the organization. One of the best ways to begin that process was to be visible on the sites and build relationships. When I assumed the role of superintendent in the fall of 2003, I established a pattern of visiting every classroom in the district at least twice a year. When Rich Smith came as an assistant superintendent, he also developed a regular pattern of visiting sites and doing classroom walk-throughs. This allowed us to spend time viewing instruction with principals and coaching them on their instructional leadership. As we started the PLC journey, our pattern of site visits continued and included reflective conversations and classroom visitations, but the focus shifted from instruction as the main focus of the visits. The site time now became a conversation about PLC progress, and classroom visitations focused on evidence of team collaboration and student learning. Instruction was still on our radar screen, but strengthening collaboration and deepening the learning of students and adults were focal points of the conversation. While Rich and I had developed strong relationships with our principals based on trust and respect, the reality was we were still the ones who, at the end of the day, were responsible for the evaluation of principal performance as well. In spite of our intentions to serve as a resource for capacity building, we could never totally escape that accountability link in our coaching work.

But we realized that building relationships also involves developing connections within the organization as well as among individuals, and this proved to be a powerful turning point. Principals began to form loose networks of support, which, in essence, became a principal team within the PLC. They met in groups and walked through classes together and shared in reflective conversations to learn with and from one another. These informal peer-to-peer chats evolved into a peer-coaching process on the elements of PLC leadership. As principals began to support one another in capacity building, their alliances developed into shared learning among schools as well. Groups of two to four schools would periodically meet after school, and their collaborative teams would meet by grade levels to share best practices and resources. As we watched these relationships develop, we realized we were seeing real evidence of the shifts referenced in the introduction (pages 5–7) and the development of another level of job-embedded learning opportunity. When we build those connections, those strong relationships within teams and sites, we strengthen the development of shared vision and mission and our commitments to achieving them.

We must also invest in building trust in our systems and, through that trust, strong relationships and connections to our work as a PLC. We have to provide access to information that helps us build shared understanding and shared beliefs. The culture of a PLC drives the work it must do; if your culture is weak, fractured, or focused on adults' needs rather than on students' learning, your outcomes will not be strong. Shaping the culture so that we all share the same values and common intent is a daily leadership action.

Chapter 2

Developing Capacity Through Distributed Leadership

The most pernicious myth about leadership is that it is reserved for only a few of us . . . leadership is accessible to anyone who has the passion and purpose to change things as they are.

—Jim Kouzes and Barry Posner

When Richard DuFour begins his presentation about leadership at a PLC Institute, he shares this definition of leadership: "Leadership is working with others to establish a shared sense of purpose, goals, and direction, and then persuading people to move in that direction" (Louis, Leithwood, Wahlstrom, & Anderson, 2010). Based on this starting point, he presents an amended definition of leadership as (Richard DuFour, 2014):

- Working with others to establish a shared sense of purpose, goals, and direction.

- Persuading people to move in that direction.

- Clarifying the steps to be taken to begin moving in the right direction.

- Providing the resources and support that enable people to succeed at what they are being asked to do.

He describes leadership as something that should be distributed throughout the system to be most effective in driving change.

The foundation of shared mission, vision, values, and goals, the clear understanding of the six characteristics of a PLC, the three big ideas, and the four key questions frame the district work and leadership tasks at all levels. Now, let's look at these leadership roles at the district, site, and team levels before we consider how you coach the capacity to lead and what that leadership role looks like.

Defining Roles of District Leadership

The role of district leadership—the superintendent, the board, the superintendent's cabinet, and all others who carry forward the work of the district in their roles—has not always been seen as having a great impact in supporting student achievement. In many cases, district leaders were so wrapped up in conducting the *busyness* of the district, they failed to understand and address the business of the district—learning! Yet researchers find that the district office's role is critical in defining and supporting the need to improve outcomes.

> A principal and key staff could help a school improve student achievement through heroic effort, but they could not sustain the improvement or survive the departure of key leaders without the support of the district and a commitment at that level to promote effective schooling practices. (Lezotte, 2008, as cited in DuFour & Marzano, 2011, p. 28)

District leadership has been found to have "a measurable effect on student achievement" (Marzano & Waters, 2009, p. 12) and to be vital in improving school systems (Louis et al., 2010; Mourshed, Chijioke, & Barber, 2010).

DuFour and Marzano (2011) describe five main points of focus for district leadership:

1. Effective district leaders both direct and empower others.

2. Effective district leaders create a common language.

3. Effective district leaders monitor the PLC process in each school as they develop principal leadership capacity.

4. Effective superintendents limit initiatives.

5. Effective superintendents communicate priorities effectively.

Direct and Empower Others

In order to be directive and empowering at the same time, it is critical that the district team from the superintendent down understands and embraces the concept of loose-tight leadership (DuFour et al., 2010) or defined autonomy (Marzano & Waters, 2009). The role of the district leadership team is to define those things that are *tight*—the non-negotiables that must be in place at the site level—and then to be *loose* in giving each site team the autonomy to build the work at the site to best meet the needs of its students using the strengths of its staff.

Create a Common Language

Clarifying the district work—the non-negotiables—creates a common language that is spoken and understood by all in the district. It is important that this language develops meaning through its use in practice; in other words, it is not the latest buzzword, but a shared vocabulary that has common meaning, as when we speak of common formative assessments or SMART goals. (Visit www.allthingsplc.info to access a glossary of terms for aiding this language development.)

Monitor the PLC Process and Develop Principal Leadership Capacity

Monitoring the PLC process, assessing progress, and addressing the capacity of the principals and their teams require district leadership to embrace reciprocal accountability:

> Accountability must be a reciprocal process. For every increment of performance I demand from you, I have an equal responsibility to provide you with the capacity to meet that expectation. Likewise, for every investment you make in my skill and knowledge, I have a reciprocal responsibility to demonstrate some new increment in performance. This is the principle of "reciprocity of accountability for capacity." It is the glue that, in the final analysis, will hold accountability systems together. (Elmore, 2000, as cited in Elmore, 2002, p. 7)

Reciprocal accountability was well understood and embraced in the work we did in Sanger (David & Talbert, 2013; Fullan, 2013). In order to support the PLC process, district leadership must be visible and engaged in the work of the sites. District leaders can't assume that the work is moving forward, and they can't determine the effectiveness of the work if their only interaction with site leaders is in isolation of the site. Knowing where sites are on the journey through regular engagement in their work and frequent site visits also helps district leadership understand where they need further support.

Limit Initiatives

The district leadership's role in removing barriers to progress is critical to forward progress. Often we create barriers in the system by failing to narrow the focus of the district's mission, vision, or goals, and the scope of the measures we implement to achieve them. We have, in our work through continuous periods of reform, tended to add programs and expectations as a response to the need for improvement in student learning outcomes. What we have not done well is ask the question, "What should we stop doing?" The ability to identify the few things that need to be done really well—building the capacity of the organization to meet those expectations within that narrowed focus—and then focusing on getting really good at those things is a pathway to improved outcomes.

Communicate Priorities Effectively

Communicating the non-negotiables loudly, regularly, and in the common language is a critical function of the superintendent's shared vision for the future. Many times, such a task has translated to sharing a powerful conversation at the start of the year—and that's it. I remember when a superintendent in our region whom I was coaching shared how excited he was about his start-of-the-year message and how he was sure it would set the right tone for the work that year. I watched as he shared a thirty-minute PowerPoint presentation highlighting all of the facilities improvements done over the summer. While his intention was to show how the district was investing in improvement, it had no correlation to the actual work of the district—the learning! Communicating the right message to the organization clearly and on an ongoing basis is an important duty of district-level leaders.

Adopt a Servant-Leader Mentality

When I first came to Sanger, principals voiced frustration over not being clear which master they really served. To them, it felt like the compliance demands from various departments at the district office kept them from being able to keep their focus on the real work of student learning. Timothy Kanold (2011) and Anthony Muhammad and Sharroky Hollie (2012) address this concern with their references to the need to develop a service or servant mentality about our roles as leaders. We must remind ourselves that ultimately the system exists for one purpose—to serve students—and that work happens at the site level. It is critical that we pose the question of all who serve at the district level: "How can we be seen as providing a service to the sites by doing everything within our power to minimize our disruptive influence at the site level?"

Our business department demonstrated a real shift to servant mentality in the way it changed its usual practice of calling principals to come into the district office to meet with staff regarding budget issues. The business office realized how much time away from the sites it demanded of the principals. To reduce this impact, the district office went to the site and met with the principals there. The time spent on the sites led to a clearer understanding of the district work by the district office business team and a greater desire to find more ways to serve the sites. If we want to build the capacity of leaders, we must start with an understanding that the role of the leader is to serve.

Defining Roles of Site Leadership

Leadership at the site level has changed dramatically. In the past, an effective principal was someone who managed his or her site well, knew the names of students, and kept problems away from the district office. The role of the principal was not really linked to learning outcomes. While an effective principal must be able to manage the operations of the school, recent research findings regarding the role of principals and their impact on student learning have changed:

> In short, a justifiable conclusion one can glean from the research is that the more skilled the building principal, the more learning can be expected among students. Stated differently, the research now supports what practitioners have known for decades: powerful school leadership on the part of the principal has a positive effect on student achievement. (DuFour & Marzano, 2011, p. 48)

The principal does not directly influence students' learning, but rather indirectly influences it through the impact of quality leadership practices on teachers. Fullan (2014) also addresses this indirect link to learning and the importance of the principal's role:

> First, this body of research establishes that groups of teachers, working together in purposeful ways over periods of time, will produce greater learning in more students. Thus, if principals directly influence how teachers can learn together, they will maximize their impact on student learning. Second, although the route to impacting student achievement is one step removed, causally speaking, it must be nonetheless explicit. If principals merely enable teachers to work together and do not help forge the final link to actual learning, the process will fail. (pp. 65–66)

Milbrey McLaughlin and Joan Talbert (2006) echo the importance of the impact that principals have: "Principals arguably are the most important players affecting the character and consequences of teachers' school-site professional communities. Principals are culture makers, intentionally or not" (as cited in DuFour & Marzano, 2011, p. 47). This statement again underscores the need to develop strong site leadership to guide the work of the learning community and therefore ensure that its influence on the culture and learning outcomes is intentional.

Site Leadership Actions to Support PLC Work

To ensure that the influence of the principal is intentional for the work of on-site teams, it is important to recognize the principal's actions that have the greatest impact on student learning outcomes. Principals must:

- Build a collaborative culture based on shared mission, vision, values, and goals and a shared commitment to achieve them

- Keep teams focused on student learning and engaged in ongoing action research regarding best practices to improve student outcomes that is driven by results

- Ensure that teams develop and work toward achieving clear SMART goals that can only be achieved through the interdependent work of collaborative teams

- Be accessible to teams, differentiate support to teams, monitor the achievement of goals, and celebrate success

Principals must build a culture of trust with the teams they lead and develop an understanding that adult learning is most powerful when it is job-embedded. This requires that we must at times take risks and that we have permission to fail, as long as we use our results to grow and learn as a team. According to DuFour et al. (2010), this job-embedded learning is also the best way to prepare the principal as well.

Site Collaborative Team Leaders

Establishing a site leadership team is an essential role of the principal to support a learning-centered focus and a collaborative culture. The principal coaches the needed skill development in his or her leadership team, and the team leaders in turn guide the work of their teams and keep the focus on learning. Ronald Gallimore, Bradley Ermeling, William Saunders, and Claude Goldenberg (2009, as cited in DuFour & Marzano, 2011) state:

> Effective principals will not attempt to do it alone. They will foster shared leadership by identifying and developing educators to lead their collaborative teams because without effective leadership at the team level, the collaborative process is likely to drift away from issues most critical to student learning. (p. 57)

This supports the essential concept of distributed leadership, underscores the continuous need to invest in building capacity, and suggests that the selection of leaders is an important function that the principal guides. DuFour and Marzano (2011) continue by sharing what they believe are four key factors to consider in that selection of teacher leaders.

1. **Their influence with colleagues:** Is this an individual whose credibility with others is so strong that his or her support for an initiative or idea will influence others in that direction?

2. **Their willingness to be a champion of the PLC process:** Is this someone who demonstrates an understanding and support of the process by modeling commitment to learning, collaboration, and a focus on results?

3. **Their sense of self-efficacy and willingness to persist:** Is this someone who understands that the solutions do not lie anywhere else but with us, who can demonstrate his or her belief that it is the collective actions of the team that will have a positive impact on results, and who will develop solutions when faced with challenges?

4. **The ability to think systematically:** Is this someone who can bring coherence to the team process by helping the team see the connection that teamwork has with improving the school and the district?

Selecting the right leaders is critical to building effective leadership teams. The principal needs to guide that selection process to ensure that the leadership team actually has the ability to provide leadership at both the team and site level.

Defining Roles of Team Leadership

The concept of distributed leadership is necessary, especially so at the site level; the principal can't do it alone. We realized this early on in the Sanger journey, and David and Talbert (2013) reflect on this shift in leadership structure at the site level:

> In every school, teachers led the grade level or course level PLCs [collaborative teams]. This is often the first opportunity teachers have to take on leadership responsibilities. To carry out this role, they must understand the purpose and function of PLCs as well as develop interpersonal skills to facilitate their teams through bumps in the road. Teacher leadership also grows through school-based leadership teams that span grade levels and content areas. (p. 24)

These leadership teams became an important link between the principals and their teams, as well as a way to facilitate both the development of shared understanding and decision making in relation to site issues. Leaders of these teams, too, play important roles.

Guiding the cultural shift to collaboration and shared understanding goes back to the foundational pillars of a PLC—mission, vision, values, and goals. The values we establish define who we must be, how we must behave so that we can work together to accomplish our mission, and how we will build our shared vision. The role of the PLC leader is critical here; the first step the team needs to guide itself through is the establishment of norms to guide team members' work together.

Hold Team Members Accountable to Norms

Norms are not rules to which the team agrees, but rather commitments that the team makes to one another that define how it will develop that sense of interdependence and mutual accountability in its collaborative work. When we began the PLC journey, we did not emphasize the importance of each collaborative team at our sites developing their own norms as a starting point on the journey. We very quickly learned we had made a mistake; without those commitments, many of our teams were really nothing more than groups that came together and lacked focus and purpose. Patrick Lencioni's

(2005) comments on norms underscore what we had failed to recognize: "One thing is certain: having clear norms gives teams a huge advantage. . . . The key to [effective teams] is involving all members in establishing the norms, and then holding everyone accountable to what they have agreed upon" (pp. 53–54). In essence, Lencioni is saying "norms can help clarify expectations, promote open dialogue, and serve as a powerful tool for holding members accountable" (Lencioni, 2005, as cited in DuFour et al., 2010, p. 144).

Six simple guidelines serve as tips for using norms (DuFour et al., 2010, p. 136):

1. Each team should create its own norms.
2. Norms should be stated as *commitments* to act or behave in a certain way rather than as beliefs.
3. Norms should be reviewed at the beginning and end of each meeting for at least six months.
4. Teams should formally evaluate their effectiveness at least twice a year.
   - Are we adhering to our norms?
   - Do we need to establish a new norm to address a problem occurring on our team?
   - Are all members of our team contributing to its work?
   - Are we working together interdependently to achieve our team goals?
5. Teams should focus on a few essential norms rather than creating an extensive laundry list!
6. Violations of team norms must be addressed.

Norms must be established; that has to be the work of each team. Once in place, the norms will guide the team leader as she or he coaches the development of the team's function and collaborative culture. The norms each team develops give the site leader guidance to coach team function, as well.

Facilitate Focus and Growth

Collaborative team leaders must also understand the growth and development of a team and the characteristics of a healthy team. A healthy team will exhibit five characteristics. They are the ability to (Lencioni, 2002):

1. Establish trust

2. Engage in honest dialogue regarding disagreements

3. Make commitments to one another

4. Hold each other accountable

5. Focus on results

Lencioni describes the dysfunctions of a team as the inability to do these five things, and so teacher leaders coaching the development of their team should be aware that their work must be centered on building trust and the understanding that a healthy team will disagree, but the team norms guide how it handles those disagreements. The teacher leader must hold the team to those commitments, establish the sense of interdependence and mutual accountability, and keep the team focused on results.

Sustaining Leadership

When leadership is widely distributed in these ways, so too is learning. *Cultures Built to Last* echoes the power of distributed leadership and the impact on a system:

> Leadership development that sustains an improvement process means giving lots of people throughout the organization both challenging experiences directly tied to the system's goals and ongoing support and feedback to develop their collective capacity to meet those challenges. People at all levels are being groomed for leadership through their work, not away from their work . . . In a system characterized by widely distributed leadership, everyone's work should be

designed to improve the capacity and performance of
someone else. (DuFour & Fullan, 2013, p. 72)

When we embrace this concept of shared leadership as a means to
develop capacity with an understanding that our job is to get better
and help others to do the same, the entire system benefits. The concept of distributed leadership creates a pipeline of potential leaders
to fill future needs at different levels throughout the organization
and also serves to develop an organizational culture and focus on
continuous improvement.

Supporting the development of leadership capacity through coaching
is only truly effective if you also have a plan for leadership development. When I arrived in Sanger in 1999, I very quickly realized that
our system really had no formal structure in place to provide leadership
opportunities or to encourage those who might have the ability to lead
to do so. Some of the principals had come up through the ranks, and
some had come to Sanger from neighboring districts as well. When
we had principal openings early on, we had some candidates with a
desire to lead and an earned credential, but little or no actual leadership
experience. We began to hire candidates from other districts who had
the necessary credentials and some level of experience. We also began
to build our own system of leader development.

Create Opportunities to Lead

None of our elementary schools had vice principals, and we had
only one middle school and one high school, so there were limited
entry-level administrative leadership opportunities available. We
developed a support position at sites throughout the district that
was almost a mentor-teacher role; we called it a curriculum support
provider (CSP). This role provides support for teachers in improving
instructional practice and understanding curriculum. We realized
that this position could serve as our entry-level leadership opportunity by strengthening the leadership role of the job and changing our
recruitment and hiring practices for the position. If your objective

is to develop future leaders in that role, it probably is not a good practice to hire well-intended and talented individuals who have no ambition to lead in any role other than that of a CSP. That does not imply that we did not hire some who we knew would only lead at that level because their skills were so deep that they would have an impact; we did. However, we also encouraged talented individuals who we knew had the desire and ability to lead at higher levels to consider moving into these positions in order to further develop their leadership capabilities.

Support Opportunities for Growth at All Career Stages

Credentialing was a concern as well. At Sanger, we did not have many teachers who were pursuing an administrative credential in preparation for future opportunity. We partnered with one of our local universities, California State University, Fresno, in several ways to solve this. Realizing that the shortage of credentialed potential administrators was a regional issue, the university approached the system chancellor with a request to start a cohort-training program that would partially fund the cost of the credential program for participating members. The chancellor agreed and thus the Chancellor's Fellows Program through its Kremen School of Education began.

Districts submitted the names of potential candidates for inclusion, and if the applicants were selected, the chancellor's support paid for half of the program cost. We actively encouraged our aspiring leaders to seek admission into the program and began to have two to three candidates accepted into each cohort. This effort was successful until budget reductions in the state forced the chancellor to eliminate the funding for the participant scholarships. However, we partnered with the university again and established cohorts of master's degree offerings in education leadership, curriculum leadership, and reading instruction. For the two-year program, the university sends professors to the district where they conduct classes in our facilities. These cohorts allowed promising candidates to network and prepare in a supportive setting, as all other participants were also district employees.

This cohort concept also shifted over into our teacher preparation and recruitment efforts as well. We are only twenty miles or so from the university, but historically, we had a hard time placing student teachers in the district. Two cohorts were already established in districts in two cities around the university, Clovis and Fresno, but none outside of that area. With the development of our professional learning community work, we approached the university with another request: place a cohort of student teachers in our district and provide their course instruction here also. We asked that placement of student teachers not be limited to a traditional master teacher focus, but rather be embedded in PLCs to experience the power of collaborative team work. This developed into a powerful capacity-building opportunity for the student teachers and a coaching opportunity for the PLC itself to aid in the development of these aspiring educators. It also provided us with a great opportunity to have potential future hires already familiar with and experienced in the work of PLCs and who had developed a clear understanding of the role of teacher leaders through this experience. These partnerships in Sanger led to the development of additional partnerships in neighboring districts; the work has been so effective that the Kremen School received national recognition for its excellence in teacher preparation.

Communicate With Sites to Identify Potential Leaders

With the development of a professional learning community in our district and the realization that distributed leadership was a critical shift in thinking and real practice, the role of teacher leaders grew in importance as the starting point for leadership development. Teacher leaders soon became the leadership development proving ground. We worked with our principals to have the right teachers in those roles. We helped principals understand their role in coaching teacher leaders on skills needed to lead the work of their teams successfully. We also solicited principals' observations about those whom they saw as having the potential and desire to lead. Rich Smith and I regularly reviewed our notes on leadership development so that we knew who was ready for a new level, who had developed potential, and those who needed a bit more time, experience, and encouragement. The development of this leadership pipeline and continuous capacity building in the district has been so effective that Sanger Unified has not filled a leadership position at any level in the district with a candidate from outside of the district since 2008. By growing our own, we had the ability to develop and deepen the culture because all new leaders understand that the work of the district is learning and their job is to be a leader of learning.

Understanding the levels of leadership—district, site, and teacher—that must be engaged in supporting the PLC work and developing capacity to meet expectations, the question now becomes, How do we do that? How do we coach to build leadership capacity that supports continuous improvement? Chapter 3 will address the structure and function of coaching.

Chapter 3
Structuring and Supporting Leadership Coaching

The only real training for leadership is leadership.

—Anthony Jay

What is coaching? How do you coach? You can find a wide variety of answers to these questions. John Wooden says, "A coach is someone who can give correction without causing resentment." A variety of online resources provide other views; take, for example, the online blog post "What Is Coaching? 10 Definitions," which includes the following (as cited in karencwise, 2010):

1. "Unlocking a person's potential to maximize their own performance. It is helping them to learn rather than teaching them." (Whitmore, 2003)

2. "A collaborative, solution-focused, results-oriented and systematic process in which the coach facilitates the enhancement of work performance, life experience, self-directed learning, and personal growth of the coachee." (Grant, 1999; basic definition also referred to by the Association for Coaching, 2005)

3. "A professional partnership between a qualified coach and an individual or team that support the achievement of extra-ordinary results, based on goals set by the individual or team." (ICF, 2005)

4. "The art of facilitating the performance, learning and development of another." (Downey, 2003)

These definitions give an overview of coaching that implies guiding improved performance and building capacity are its aims, but they also illuminate the nature and aims of coaching—to generate learning and to be collaborative, results-oriented, solution-focused, and systematic—based on goals the individual or team sets. I really like the fourth definition the best as it implies that means other than direct interaction will serve as coaching structures and supports.

Facilitating the performance, learning, and development of others in our schools and systems requires that we invest in the development of what Fullan and Hargreaves (2012) call *professional capital*. Professional capital is a combination of three things:

1. **Human capital**—Building the skills and capacity of individuals; coaching one to one has impact here, but you can't invest all your efforts on this level because you can't change culture on an individual basis.

2. **Social capital**—We invest in building the quality and capacity of the group, a collaborative effort where we work together to improve our collective capabilities to improve learning outcomes for all kids.

3. **Decisional capital**—Building our access to data and ability to use data to drive our improvement in a constant "ready-fire-aim" cycle of system learning. The ready-fire-aim mantra is Fullan's version of a cycle of inquiry and continuous improvement. We see a problem (ready); we take action (fire); we analyze our results (aim) to identify the next thing we see we need to act on. When we use ready-fire-aim, we sometimes

spend so much time analyzing things and admiring the problem (aiming) that we often don't get to action (fire).

Coaching to develop professional capital requires that we establish systems and structures that create coaching conversations and opportunities among leaders at all levels on a regular basis. Those coaching conversations flow in all directions in the organization. Kanold (2011) describes this as cultivating an N-S-E-W sphere of influence. He says, "You can choose to lead *north* to those who have positional authority over you, *south* to those entrusted to your leadership, or *east* or *west* to those who are your lateral peers" (Kanold, 2011, p. 85). Leading works in all four directions; coaching leadership in all four directions is a requirement in order to build a learning system, to become a PLC on a systemwide scale.

Elements of Coaching

So what are the elements of coaching that we need to be aware of and need to consider when investing in the building of leadership capacity? In *Leadership Coaching*, authors Donald Wise and Marc Hammack (2011) summarize their research on the subject by grouping coaching competencies into four categories for discussion.

1. Establishing the coaching relationship
2. Communicating effectively
3. Facilitating learning and performance
4. Using best practices

The authors repeatedly refer to the need for coaching to be based on a relationship of trust and confidentiality. Conversations between coach and coachee must stay between them for the process to be effective; the coach becomes a non-evaluative set of eyes and ears to share learning and build leadership skills. This is critical to understand and support. In a recent conversation I had with a young principal, he mentioned his supervisor informed him in his first year as a principal that the purpose of their time spent together was to build his leadership capacity and provide him with coaching. As a result, the principal shared areas in which he was having difficulties in an effort to seek help, only to find that at the end of the year he had been flagged and called out for areas of weakness in his evaluation for every struggle he shared. Needless to say, his trust in the relationship vanished, and this principal is still dealing with the damage from that violation of trust.

The coach must be an effective communicator, meaning he or she must skillfully pose reflective questions to generate learning through the process and must also be a great listener. Listening in this context means more than hearing what is said but also being able to read the nonverbal messages being sent through body language, gestures, and expressions. Coaches must be able to help their coachee establish goals and monitor progress as well as manage change. They also assist in the identification of *best practices*—highly effective strategies or initiatives that help drive improved outcomes.

Resources for Coaching

Regardless of the purpose of the coaching, identifying coaches who can individualize support is essential to successful leadership development. If a district's budget allows, a full-time coaching team is a possible solution to consider. Large districts are more likely to have the human resources available from which to draw to support this work, but all of us must examine the resources, both financial and human, we have available or that can be redirected to support this work.

Utilizing External Coaching Supports

Our first efforts at coaching required outside resources and expertise. We partnered with the Pivot Learning Partners (then called Bay Area School Reform Collaborative) to begin the coaching process. We had several principals at a variety of experience levels whom we thought would benefit from having a coach. In meeting with Pivot Learning Partners to discuss supports, its coaching structure had all of the elements we needed; it was formed on a relationship of trust and confidentiality, provided experienced coaches who were effective communicators, and focused on learning through reflective conversations and problem solving linked to best practice. The coaching sessions, which were held on site and included classroom visits, centered on improving instruction and collaborative practice to advance student learning. Pivot Learning Partners also provided superintendent coaching as a component of its package.

Along with another superintendent and colleague of mine, I engaged in reflective conversations with our coach, Walt Buster, who had recently retired as a very successful superintendent. With a focus on our goals to improve student learning outcomes and close our achievement gap, he coached us in building capacity, improving instruction, and developing a collaborative culture. Sometimes we met for breakfast; other times, we would visit a site and walk through classrooms with the principal, after which we would reflect on what we had seen and heard, the strengths of what we had observed, and noted opportunities for growth. These conversations mirrored the coaching conversations our principals were having; for me, I gained unique insight from having a peer engaged in the conversation with our coach and me. Very quickly, what developed was a pattern of *peer-coaching conversations* on the learning and applications. This helped me understand that while individual coaching is one element of building leadership capacity, there are many more ways to *coach* the development of leadership. The peer-to-peer collaborative learning conversation was definitely one very powerful additional strategy we needed to include in some way when developing our capacity to build and support leadership at all levels.

Finding Support From Within

Unfortunately, most of us do not fall into the category of large districts, and finding resources to fund extras can be problematic.

Creative utilization of existing resources becomes the solution. At Sanger, we shifted from relying on external support to drawing on internal resources—our leaders themselves. Our most pressing need was the support of leaders new in their roles, especially principals. Our answer? Use our team to support our team. We assigned a coach or mentor to each new principal. This was usually someone from the central office team who had been a successful site leader and effective in guiding his or her site's PLC work. Sometimes the coach was another principal who would agree to provide support. This provided the opportunity to have growth conversations and coaching opportunities with someone who knew the journey but was not linked to the evaluation loop. The support included on-site conversations and check-in by phone on a regular basis. The collaborative culture of the district enabled the rapid establishment of an informal network of coaching support through peers.

Coaching new principals ensured their success and supported their growth, but what about the rest of the team? My own experience as a coachee helped me understand the value of coaching and see the need to provide as many opportunities as possible for support. To expand our ability to offer it, we again focused on existing resources. We considered the function and structure of the existing central office team. To support capacity building and, to an extent, succession development, we restructured roles to create new positions eventually called Area Administrators, or AAs. Each of the AAs had oversight of various district programs and between them, oversight of all sites in the district, but none had evaluation responsibilities. The AAs functioned as a team and met regularly to support one another and coordinate efforts. They regularly met with all site principals and to walk through classrooms, and they guided subsequent learning conversations using reflective questioning focused on improvement. The AAs would also connect groups of principals to reflect on best practices observed at the host site and generate shared learning through those conversations. The AAs' work proved to be a tremendous support in building leadership capacity and became a source of job-embedded learning for individuals in that role—so much so that one of the original AAs is the current associate superintendent for curriculum and instruction and another is the current superintendent.

With the success of our efforts to support coaching using our own resources, we again turned our attention to how we provide training in the district. Districtwide efforts at professional development were exactly that, professional development districtwide! This approach had its drawbacks. For example, we trained every teacher in the district in our instructional platform, but it took three years to complete the process for the first cycle of training.

We began to rethink this method shortly after I had the opportunity to spend some time in Toronto with members of the Stuart Foundation board. Responding to the lackluster impact of professional development delivered as an isolated event, I heard Michael Fullan (2012) remark there that professional development is a great way to avoid change; we need professional learning. The facts show declining evidence of knowledge and impact on practice over time. Fullan (2014) again references this concern about professional development versus professional learning when he cites the work of Peter Cole (2004, 2013). The failure of professional development to drive change in performance is linked to our failure to create a culture of learning in our systems. We tend to focus on what we have done to provide training rather than asking what changed because of the training we did. This thinking was a part of our shift in training to increase *professional learning* and the capacity of leadership teams.

We began a cohort-training model in which principals and leadership teams from various sites in the district convened in cohorts to discuss and learn new thinking or strategies. The site-leadership teams were then responsible for sharing the learning with others at their sites. PLC team leaders would share the learning within the team and link student outcomes to new thinking or strategies. The leadership teams from the cohort sites shared what they learned with the rest of the cohort teams, which then accelerated learning across the district. Capacity building, connecting peers with purpose, learning as the work, system learning—all are connected through a shift in practice that creates internal coaching and learning capacity.

Chapter 4
Coaching Leadership to Sustain PLCs

Information is not knowledge.

—Albert Einstein

In the context of PLCs, coaches often help coachees develop their leadership capacity in relation to the three big ideas and four key questions that frame and guide the work of PLCs. Coaching leadership in a PLC becomes a function of the system. When we understand that, in a professional learning community, coaching becomes the work of our system, whether that is as a site or as a district, we all are leaders of learning, and we learn by doing. Coaching leadership development is not just what a *coach* does; we all become coaches as we learn together.

Coaching to Lead Learning

The first big idea that guides PLC work is a relentless focus on learning. Well, of course, you say; it is school, after all, and learning is what happens there. Unfortunately for too many students, the time spent in school has not resulted in learning because the structures, support, and belief system necessary to ensure that all students learn are not in place. What does it mean to have a learning-centered focus? It starts with the development of a shared vision and commitment that ensure that school is a place where learning for all is reality. That is the job of leadership, and leadership is a shared responsibility distributed throughout members of the team.

Clearly, leaders at district, site, and team levels have tremendous potential to impact students' learning. As the Center for Educational Leadership (CEL) at the University of Washington (2014a) states:

> Among school-related factors, school leadership is second only to teaching in its potential influence on student learning. Instructional leadership is a critical aspect of school leadership. The work of instructional leaders is to ensure that each student receives the highest quality instruction each day. Doing so requires instructional leaders lead for the improvement of the quality of teaching and for the improvement of student learning. (p. 1)

Good teaching does matter, and it is reported to be the most important factor of influence on student learning. It is, therefore, important that we coach the capability of every teacher to be able to deliver high-quality instruction every day. Research supports the importance of good teaching, even to the point of tying the effectiveness of a whole system to the quality of its teaching. As Barber and Mourshed (2009) note, "There is no more important empirical determinant of student outcomes than good teaching. Second only to the quality of teaching is school leadership" (p. 27). In essence, they have found that the quality of the education system cannot exceed the quality of its teachers. The only way to improve outcomes is to improve teaching, and to improve teaching, we must build capacity in our leaders.

When shifting one's thinking about coaching, you will find that research commonly discusses instructional leadership either in the context of coaching of teachers in their instruction or in supporting the development of principals as *instructional leaders*. Leadership capacity building in a PLC requires a more multifaceted approach, but elements of the instructional-leader platform of coaching are helpful here. As a starting point, consider DuFour and Fullan's (2013) concept of right and wrong drivers. They define a driver as:

> A policy intended to have a positive impact on a particular domain, such as student learning. For example, policies that are based on punitive accountability are less effective in promoting student learning than policies that focus on developing new capacities (like endorsing PLCs). (p. 22)

Fullan (2013) identifies four drivers he considers to have the right impact on student learning and four that serve as wrong drivers in their overall impact (see table 4.1).

Table 4.1: Right and Wrong Drivers

Wrong Drivers	Right Drivers
Accountability	Capacity building
Human capital (the talent of the individual)	Social capital (the quality of the group)
Technology	Instruction
Fragmented strategies	Systems

Each of the right drivers supports the shifts that are needed to build strong PLCs and a collaborative culture. In my own journey in leadership, I spent a lot of time and effort in my role as the assistant superintendent for human resources, reminding principals that the purpose of evaluations is to guide the improvement of employee performance, which in turn generates better learning outcomes for students. This was the right message, but evaluations are in fact an accountability measure and a compliance activity. In far too many cases, the evaluation may be based on a one-time visit to a classroom, which is usually a staged dog-and-pony show for the observer. Even if the process includes multiple observations with reflective conversations, the end product only centers on one individual's work and may not result in any significant improvement in the employee's performance or student learning outcomes. While the evaluation process (accountability) is required by law, a much greater impact on learning should occur if the principal invests time in developing social capital, working with PLCs in linking achieved outcomes to strategies used to improve instructional practice. These right drivers provide the foundation for coaching to develop leadership at all levels of PLC work.

Coaching to Improve the Collaborative Culture

Norms help develop team commitments, and goals provide the benchmarks for monitoring expectations and results, but leaders must also be aware of who the players on the team are. Every team is made up of individuals who approach change in different ways; some will be on board with a new idea quickly, others take a bit more convincing, and still others will resist change. To effectively move PLCs forward, principals must know their team well enough that they know how to support and coach their teacher leaders in team dynamics. In his book *Transforming School Culture*, Anthony Muhammad (2009) gives a very clear and helpful overview of the types of individuals we find in our work. He says that you will find four groups: (1) believers, (2) tweeners, (3) survivors, and (4) fundamentalists. They can all be present in your teams, and you need to know who they are, their impact on your culture, and how to guide each of them to a point of being a contributing member of your team.

Believers

Believers are educators who believe in the core values that make up a healthy school culture. They believe that all of their students are capable of learning and that they have direct impact on success (Muhammad, 2009). The believers are more than likely the ones who you draw on as your teacher leaders, within your PLC, and as members of your site-leadership team. They see and share the vision and believe in the students they serve.

Tweeners

Tweeners are educators who are new to the school culture. Their experience can be likened to a honeymoon period in which they spend time trying to learn the norms and expectations of the school's culture (Muhammad, 2009). Your tweeners are the team members who are still developing their own beliefs, and their experience during this honeymoon period will influence this development. Supporting tweeners and coaching them are critical to shaping them into believers rather than fundamentalists. The coaching support of both the site leaders as well as the team members with whom they work is important in guiding them into the right belief system. Site leaders need to know the dynamics of the teams into which they are placing folk; knowing the dynamics will help them know when they need to support the team leader in coaching, or when they need to be the coach. Early in our journey, we had a team that really had no clear leadership and was struggling to find its path. The principal invested in supporting and coaching a second-year teacher who, while essentially a tweener, with the right support would not only shift roles, but would also develop as a leader. He convinced her to take over leadership of this team and continued to support her in this new leadership role and coach her in guiding the team. Not only did she quickly shift into the role of absolute believer, but she also learned to lead by leading, the best way to build leadership capacity.

By the end of that year, this team had developed into one of the strongest at its site, and its outcomes for students were incredible.

Survivors

The third group is the survivors, a small group of teachers who are burned out, so overwhelmed by the demands of the profession that they suffer from depression and merely survive from day to day (Muhammad, 2009). These are challenging folk, but I have seen even teachers who were hanging on for "one more year" show improvement through the support of a collaborative team helping them see "we are in this together."

Fundamentalists

Fundamentalists are the fourth group. Fundamentalists are staff members who are not only opposed to change, but organize to resist and thwart any change initiative. They can wield tremendous political power and are major obstacles in implementing meaningful school reform. They fall into four subgroups or levels (Muhammad, 2009):

- **Level one fundamentalists**—They resist change because they have never been provided with a clear rationale for change.

- **Level two fundamentalists**—They resist change because they do not trust the judgment or skills of their leader.

- **Level three fundamentalists**—They resist change because they are unsure if the change will cause them more stress and perhaps still not achieve a better result than current methodology.

- **Level four fundamentalists**—They resist change because change may mean admitting failure. Their reputation is based on resistance.

Understanding the why behind the resistance of a fundamentalist is critical to coaching the shift in belief and behavior needed to have him or her function in a team. Clearly communicating the case for change and soliciting fellow teachers to build the rationale with peers will help fundamentalists begin the journey to believer. Principals as learning leaders who not only lead the learning but demonstrate that they are learners as well will help build their belief in leadership and willingness to change. Building strong support around the resisters and helping them see that working as a team is actually less stressful, more productive, rewarding, and rejuvenating will shift another group of resisters. For that last group, sometimes you simply have to say, "This is what is required of you and who you will be in this work!"

I can remember two occasions where I had a conversation with fundamentalists; in both cases, after all other approaches at coaching a change in their behavior had failed, I simply said, "I get it. I don't own your beliefs, but I do rent your behavior, and from 7:30 to 3:30, this is who I need you to be and what I need you to do. After 3:30 who you are is up to you, but on my dime, this is who you will be!" This may sound drastic, but it resulted in change over time and a shift to a much more positive behavior and belief system. In both cases, they became a part of the team.

One leader had a couple of strong fundamentalists on her team. They would continually throw roadblocks in the way of team development, such as "The contract doesn't require . . . ," "My prep time is for me . . . ," and "I don't think I have to . . . ." In every case of resistance, the young developing teacher leader countered with, "Maybe not, but *our* kids need us to . . ." Her principal coached her in developing insights into why some of those arguments were the result of beliefs or experience and helped her reflect on how to reshape those beliefs and change the experience. His advice to her was to stay on message. When confronted with "adult" issues, remind the team of the norms they have developed and the commitments they have made to one another. Keep learning at the center of the team conversations and focus on results. He also suggested that if she could seek out ways to draw her fundamentalists into the conversation by drawing on their years of experience and seeking input regarding strategies to use, they might begin to soften their resistance. She took that advice and continued to draw the team back to discussions anchored in the evidence of student learning data to move the team forward. She would regularly begin the conversations by reminding the team they were here to focus on improving student learning. Ultimately, it was the focus on sharing and comparing data together and linking those outcomes to the instructional strategies that had been used in each classroom that turned the tide for the team. By the end of the year, the resisters were some of the strongest contributors on the team. Those contributions included volunteering to cover a team member's class during prep so that they could observe another team member teaching. That young teacher grew so much in her leadership capacity role that she soon became a vice principal and is now a principal, building a system of distributed leadership on her site and coaching to build the capacity of others through her leadership.

Know your players and use the team to change the team; build a collaborative culture. When dealing with resisters, always focus on the behavior, not the person, an important thing to remember when coaching others and when building the capacity of others to coach as well.

Coaching to Focus on Results Orientation

Goals serve as a method for each team to keep its focus on results, and the development of SMART goals helps keep teams focused on increasing student outcomes. The SMART goal acronym (O'Neill & Conzemius, 2006) provides an easy way to remember the goal-setting process; goals are said to be SMART when they are (DuFour et al., 2010):

- **S**trategic (aligned with the organization's goals) and specific
- **M**easurable
- **A**ttainable
- **R**esults oriented
- **T**ime bound

Monitoring the SMART goals PLCs set and providing feedback and coaching about team beliefs and expectations will ensure that adult beliefs support the district's vision of all students learning at high levels. When I interviewed Christy Platt, then teacher and team leader at a district school, about her leadership roles, she shared a story of one coaching moment her principal provided her team. The team was meeting with the principal regarding its results from a recent common formative assessment and from the District Progress Assessment. After discussing the learning journey ahead, the team reviewed the plans for the next unit of instruction. Team members had set a SMART goal as a team that after two weeks of instruction, no less than 60 percent of their students would be proficient in the new learning as measured by the common formative assessment the team developed. When questioned about the target of 60 percent proficient, the team explained that the standard it was focusing on was tough and they expected students would struggle. The principal responded to the team that he was OK with the 60 percent target as long as each of the members pulled out their grade books and identified which eight of their twenty first graders in each class would not be successful at the end of two weeks of learning. Secondly, he would expect each of them to call the parents of each of those students that night and explain to them that they were beginning a new unit of instruction and at the end of two weeks it had been decided their student would not be successful. The team was a bit shaken at first, and then realized that he was right—it was starting the learning journey with the assumption that only six out of ten students would be successful, and that adult belief and expectation would probably yield that result. Needless to say, the team modified its goal and expectations. By working with the team through its SMART goal process, the principal's coaching became a powerful learning moment for that team.

While our goal for student learning is that all students learn at high levels, it is not reasonable to write SMART goals that 100 percent will be successful. Some students will need more time and support to master the learning and need another opportunity to demonstrate that they have achieved mastery. Rich Smith coaches teams to think about a two-part SMART goal, such as "At the end of eight days' instruction on (the essential learning you are focusing on), no less than 80 percent of our students will demonstrate proficiency as measured by our common formative assessment, and at the end of three days of additional instruction, no less than 95 percent of those students not demonstrating proficiency originally will demonstrate mastery as measured by our common formative assessment." This double commitment sets a high team expectation for initial performance and a commitment by the team to provide extra time and support for learning, and an additional opportunity to demonstrate learning has occurred for the students who struggled initially. Goal setting is a great way to coach teams about expectations and beliefs and a great tool to keep teams focused on outcomes.

Monitoring Progress

We have all, I am sure, heard the statement "What gets monitored gets done." While this is a statement anchored in compliance, that starting point is sometimes necessary. The power of a learning journey takes you from a compliance starting point to a capacity-building walk. At Sanger, that became the case in coaching leadership. To focus the work of our PLCs, the district developed a very basic agenda-planning tool and required that every principal use this tool to monitor team growth and to provide feedback. The form included the four key PLC questions (see pages 4–5) and general information, such as *members present*. At first, collaborative team leaders submitted the form to their principal after every meeting. When teacher leaders from each collaborative team met with the principal to review the progress of their teams, the principal used data from the meeting records to help coach his or her leaders on deepening the level of the work and strengthening the function of the teams. They reviewed the formative assessments the team developed and discussed the level of rigor and alignment with the essential learnings upon which they were focusing. They also reviewed data from recent formative assessments and the responses to learning needs the teams were carrying out. The lead teachers then used these coaching pointers to guide the team and keep them focused on learning and results. By sharing data from a formative assessment for every student, teachers would see their results in comparison to one another. They would link the evidence of student outcomes to teaching strategies, which became a sharing of best instructional practice within the collaborative team. Analyzing the data in this way helped teachers look for trends among students who struggled and strengths of those who did well to better understand the learning needs of their collective group of students. Guided by the team leader or by the principal on those occasions when he or she met with the whole team, these conversations served to improve instructional skills of all team members.

As the function of our teams strengthened, an interesting shift happened. Principals began to hear from their teams that the district form was too basic to meet their needs. Principals in turn asked if they had to use the district form or if they could develop their own forms to better support and guide the work of the teams. Again the concept of loose-tight leadership emerged; we felt it was necessary to document teams' work, so we shifted from compliance mode to capacity mode. Site teams discussed what information needed to be included in a planning tool and began to build their own forms. These conversations and the work of the teams were a coaching opportunity for principals and lead teachers alike, and the forms developed served as a coaching guide and tool. The teams developed tools such as data analysis linking outcomes to teaching strategies, reteaching strategies, and thoughts for next steps.

The tools became a resource that helped teams collect data to monitor student learning and also became a reference resource for planning the same learning for the next year. Today, this process has evolved to the point that the teams record their meeting work on Google Docs and principals can provide real-time feedback as teams work. Every site's teamwork is accessible to all other teams at that site, which generates even deeper ongoing vertical articulation discussions between teams—another source of coaching capacity building!

Another simple tool that became a resource for coaching was a flowchart developed to show the flow of each team's work in answering the four key questions of a PLC (see figure 4.1).

Follow these steps to guide your use of the flowchart in figure 4.1:

1. What do we want all students to learn?

    - Identify essential standards.

    - Understand (unpack) each standard.

2. How will we know that learning has occurred?

    - Develop common formative assessment.

    - Set SMART goal.

    - Deliver lesson.

    - Check for understanding.

    - Appropriately adjust instruction.

    - Give common assessment.

    - Analyze data.

    - Plan based on common assessment results.

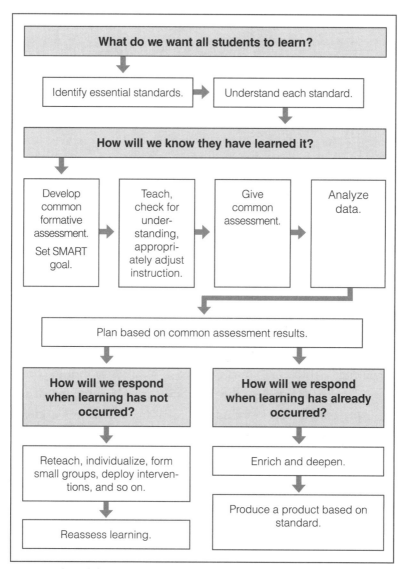

Source: Adapted from DuFour, DuFour, Eaker, & Karhanek, Raising the Bar and Closing the Gap: Whatever It Takes, *2010, pp. 26–35.*

Figure 4.1: Answering the four key questions of a PLC.

3. How do we respond when learning has not occurred?

   - Reteach, individualize, form small groups, deploy interventions, and so on.

   - Reassess learning.

4. How will we respond when learning has already occurred?

   - Enrich and deepen the learning for those who have been successful.

   - Produce a product based on standard.

While simple in format, the flowchart served as a powerful visual reminder for guiding reflection and a roadmap for progress. We were constantly reminded of the need to ensure each student would experience the guaranteed, viable curriculum. It helped remind us that if we are going to teach with the end in mind, we need to develop our measure of learning and a clear definition of proficiency *before* we begin the instructional journey. Used as a reflective tool in coaching, it kept us focused on the commitment to learning for all and on using data to support students' learning, whether that meant providing extra time and intervention, or extending opportunities for deeper engagement.

Developing leadership in a PLC requires that we establish and understand that we all lead, that we all are learners, and that we all model what is expected of us. The most powerful form of coaching we can provide with our leadership is by the example of leadership we model for them, from the superintendent to the teacher leader.

Chapter 5
Continuing the Journey

Don't let schooling interfere with your education!

—Mark Twain

So the question that I have hopefully posed in your thinking about coaching leadership is, Do you coach by leading or lead by coaching? I believe the answer is both. All levels of leadership have a shared sense of mission, vision, values, and goals that are crystal clear, demonstrated throughout the system, and visible and evident in the leadership actions we see and conversations we hear. The best way to develop leadership is by leading. The way we build our system's leadership capacity is by creating opportunities to lead and encourage and develop leadership in a shared learning journey.

That is the journey I shared for fourteen years with an incredible group of people. That is the transformation of which I was a part, the culture that I helped shape, and the team that I helped coach. The outcome of that journey is incredible both in terms of student and adult learning. We began the journey as one of the first ninety-eight school districts flagged in California for Program Improvement. Within two years, we had exited PI status. Every PI school exited within four years. Our achievement ranked in the bottom 10 percent of the state, and now the district's achievement gains have consistently ranked as some of the best in the state. Our ELs are outperforming the state averages in all areas, and our redesignated fluent EL students are the highest-performing group in the district. The district has garnered twenty State Distinguished School Designations, eighteen Title I Academic Achieving school designations, three National Blue Ribbon Schools awards, and every school with a middle school program has been recognized as a National Middle School to Watch. The cohort dropout rate of our high school students at Sanger High is at 1 percent and graduation rate at 98 percent. The outcomes for students have been incredible, and so too is the journey that continues.

Whether you lead a team in a PLC, a site as a principal, or a district as a superintendent, take action to develop the structures and systems that develop capacity. Become a leader of learning by being a leader that learns and share your learning with others. Invest in shaping your culture on an ongoing basis that includes building strong relationships anchored in trust. Believe in your students, and then act like you believe in your students. Set clear expectations and ensure that you build the capacity to meet those expectations. Develop clarity about your shared mission, vision, values, and goals, which will guide your actions and decisions as a leader and as a system. Ensure that your identity is anchored in and defined by a set of core values, your guiding principles that define who you are as a people. May that identity be so strong that your district, too, becomes a place where ordinary people do extraordinary things!

We began our journey with a conversation led by Richard DuFour and Rebecca DuFour. Our learning and actions as a district were driven by that conversation and anchored in their vision of what a professional learning community must be. It is only appropriate that we close this book with a thought from their writings regarding the identity I just described:

Clearly, the Sanger mantra—1) the job of every person in this district is to ensure student learning, 2) hoping things will get better is not a strategy, 3) don't blame the kids, and 4) the best strategy for sustained, substantive improvement is developing our capacity to work as members of a professional learning community— has benefited the students served by this district. May that mantra become the norm in districts across North America. (DuFour, DuFour, Eaker, & Karhanek, 2010, p. 162)

References and Resources

Barber, M., & Mourshed, M. (2009, July 7). *Shaping the future: How good education systems can become great in the decade ahead* (Report on the International Education Roundtable). Accessed at www.eurekanet.ru/res_ru/0_hfile_1906_1.pdf on January 16, 2015.

Center for Educational Leadership, University of Washington. (2014a). *4 dimensions of instructional leadership: Instructional Leadership Framework 1.0.* Seattle, WA: Author.

Center for Educational Leadership, University of Washington. (2014b). *Principal support framework.* Seattle, WA: Author.

Christensen, J. (Director & Producer). (1998). *FISH!* [VHS]. Burnsville, MN: ChartHouse Learning.

Cole, P. (2004). *Professional development: A great way to avoid change.* Seminar Series 194. Melbourne, Victoria, Australia: Centre for Strategic Education.

Cole, P. (2013). *Aligning professional learning, performance management and effective teaching.* Seminar Series 217. Melbourne, Victoria, Australia: Centre for Strategic Education.

David, J. L., & Talbert, J. E. (2013). *Turning around a high-poverty district: Learning from Sanger.* San Francisco: Cowell Foundation.

DuFour, R. [Rebecca]. (2014, August 14). *First things first: Building the solid foundation of a Professional Learning Community at Work™*. Keynote at Professional Learning Communities at Work Institute, Grand Rapids, Michigan.

DuFour, R. (2002). The learning-centered principal. *Educational Leadership, 59*(8), 12–15.

DuFour, R. (2005, August 12). *Building professional learning communities*. Keynote address at Professional Learning Communities Institute for Riverside County, Palm Desert, California.

DuFour, R. [Richard]. (2014, July 16). *Leaders wanted: Keys to effective leadership in Professional Learning Communities at Work*. Keynote address at PLC Institute, San Antonio, Texas.

DuFour, R., DuFour, R., Eaker, R., & Karhanek, G. (2010). *Raising the bar and closing the gap: Whatever it takes*. Bloomington, IN: Solution Tree Press.

DuFour, R., DuFour, R., Eaker, R., & Many, T. W. (2010). *Learning by doing: A handbook for professional learning communities at work* (2nd ed.). Bloomington, IN: Solution Tree Press.

DuFour, R., & Fullan, M. (2013). *Cultures built to last: Systemic PLCs at work*. Bloomington, IN: Solution Tree Press.

DuFour, R., & Marzano, R. J. (2011). *Leaders of learning: How district, school, and classroom leaders improve student achievement*. Bloomington, IN: Solution Tree Press.

Elmore, R. F. (2000). *Building a new structure for school leadership* [White paper]. Washington, DC: The Albert Shanker Institute.

Elmore, R. F. (2002). *Bridging the gap between standards and achievement: The imperative for professional development* [White paper]. Washington, DC: The Albert Shanker Institute.

Elmore, R. F. (2004). *School reform from the inside out: Policy, practice, and performance*. Cambridge, MA: Harvard Education Press.

Fullan, M. (2007). *Great to excellent: Launching the next stage of Ontario's education agenda*. Accessed at www.edu.gov.on.ca/eng /document/reports/FullanReport_EN_07.pdf on January 16, 2015.

Fullan, M. (2008). *The six secrets of change: What the best leaders do to help their organizations survive and thrive*. San Francisco, CA: Jossey-Bass.

Fullan, M. (2013). *Motion leadership in action: More skinny on becoming change savvy*. Thousand Oaks, CA: Corwin Press.

Fullan, M. (2014). *The principal: Three keys to maximizing impact.* San Francisco, CA: Jossey-Bass.

Fullan, M., & Hargreaves, A. (2012). *Professional capital: Transforming teaching in every school.* New York: Teachers College Press.

Goleman, D. (2000, March–April). Leadership that gets results. *Harvard Business Review,* pp. 78–90.

Kanold, T. D. (2011). *The five disciplines of PLC leaders.* Bloomington, IN: Solution Tree Press.

karencwise. (2010, May 20). *What is coaching? 10 definitions* [Web log post]. Accessed at https://karenwise.wordpress.com/2010/05/20/what-is-coaching-10-definitions/ on January 16, 2015.

Kouzes, J. M., & Posner, B. Z. (2010). *The truth about leadership: The no-fads, heart-of-the matter facts you need to know.* San Francisco, CA: Jossey-Bass.

Lencioni, P. (2002). *The five dysfunctions of a team: A leadership fable.* San Francisco, CA: Jossey-Bass.

Lencioni, P. (2005). *Overcoming the five dysfunctions of a team: A field guide for leaders, managers, and facilitators.* San Francisco, CA: Jossey-Bass.

Lezotte, L. W. (2008). *Effective schools: Past, present, and future.* Okemos, MI: Effective Schools Products. Accessed at www.effectiveschools.com/images/stories/brockpaper.pdf on January 21, 2011.

Louis, K. S., Leithwood, K., Wahlstrom, K. L., & Anderson, S. E. (2010). *Learning from leadership: Investigating the links to improved student learning* (Final report of research findings). Accessed at www.wallacefoundation.org/knowledge-center/school-leadership/key-research/Documents/Investigating-the-Links-to-Improved-Student-Learning.pdf on January 16, 2015.

Marzano, R. J., & Waters, T. (2009). *District leadership that works: Striking the right balance.* Bloomington, IN: Solution Tree Press.

Marzano, R. J., Waters, T., & McNulty, B. A. (2005). *School leadership that works: From research to results.* Alexandria, VA: Association for Supervision and Curriculum Development.

McLaughlin, M. W., & Talbert, J. E. (2006). *Building school-based teacher learning communities: Professional strategies to improve student achievement.* New York, NY: Teachers College Press.

Mourshed, M., Chijioke, C., & Barber, M. (2010). *How the world's most improved school systems keep getting better.* New York: McKinsey. Accessed at www.mckinsey.com/client_service /social_sector/latest_thinking/worlds_most_improved_schools on January 21, 2011.

Muhammad, A. (2009). *Transforming school culture: How to overcome staff division.* Bloomington, IN: Solution Tree Press.

Muhammad, A., & Hollie, S. (2012). *The will to lead, the skill to teach: Transforming schools at every level.* Bloomington, IN: Solution Tree Press.

No Child Left Behind (NCLB) Act of 2001, Pub. L. No. 107-110, § 115 Stat. 1425 (2002).

O'Neill, J., & Conzemius, A. (2006). *The power of SMART goals: Using goals to improve student learning.* Bloomington, IN: Solution Tree Press.

Wise, D., & Hammack, M. (2011). Leadership coaching: Coaching competencies and best practices. *Journal of School Leadership, 21*(3), 449–477.

Ybarra, S., & Hollingsworth, J. (2009). *Explicit direct instruction (EDI): The power of the well-crafted, well-taught lesson.* Thousand Oaks, CA: Corwin Press.

Zuieback, S. (2012). *Leadership practices for challenging times: Principles, skills and processes that work.* Grants Pass, OR: DG Creative.

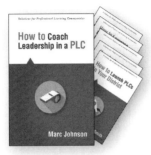

Solutions for Professional Learning Communities

The *Solutions Series* offers practitioners easy-to-implement recommendations on each book's topic—professional learning communities, digital classrooms, or modern learning. In a short, reader-friendly format, these how-to guides equip K–12 educators with the tools they need to take their school or district to the next level.

How to Use Digital Tools to Support Teachers in a PLC
William M. Ferriter
BKF675

How to Leverage PLCs for School Improvement
Sharon V. Kramer
BKF668

How to Coach Leadership in a PLC
Marc Johnson
BKF667

How to Develop PLCs for Singletons and Small Schools
Aaron Hansen
BKF676

How to Cultivate Collaboration in a PLC
Susan K. Sparks and Thomas W. Many
BKF678

How to Launch PLCs in Your District
W. Richard Smith
BKF665

"Tremendous, tremendous, tremendous!

The speaker made me do some very deep internal reflection about the **PLC process** and the personal responsibility I have in making the school improvement process work **for ALL kids**."

PD Services

Our experts draw from decades of research and their own experiences to bring you practical strategies for building and sustaining a high-performing PLC. You can choose from a range of customizable services, from a one-day overview to a multiyear process.

Book your PLC PD today!
888.763.9045

Solution Tree